Our Animal Friends

Book 5 Bailey, the Bunny Friends

James Benedict

THIS BOOK BELONGS TO:

_____

ISBN 978-1-959895-17-6 (paperback)
ISBN 978-1-959895-16-9 (ebook)

Copyright © 2022 by James Benedict

All rights reserved. No part of this publication may be reproduced, distributed, or transmitted in any form or by any means, including photocopying, recording, or other electronic or mechanical methods without the prior written permission of the publisher.

Printed in the United States of America

Sunrise brings a new day in the forest of plenty.

All the animals of the forest were abruptly awakened by a strange noise.

Ricardo the rooster gave a mighty cock-a-doodle-doo!

The noise startled all the animals of the forest.

I am visiting your country with my cousin Pauletta the porcupine from Chile. We are here with our friends Lana the llama from Peru and Giuseppe the guinea pig from Bolivia whom you have already met on a previous trip. Do you know where Brazil and Chile are located?

Brady the ground hog tells us to follow the arrows to find the locations of Brazil and Chile. These are two more countries in South America. We have already learned where Peru and Bolivia are located. Can you find them on the map.

Immigration is good for America for it makes our country stronger, wiser and better. We can live, work, pray and play together!

Bailey the bunny and Brady the ground hog came up with a good idea to celebrate their new found friendship.

All of the animal friends liked the idea of having a picnic.

Hunter the hawk called to the rest of the animals to come and enjoy the picnic and meet our new friends.

The animals played some music and Pauletta and Hunter danced, but Hunter kept backing into the porcupine and all anybody heard was, "Cha – Cha – ouch- Cha – Cha – ouch!"

Franklin the frog wanted to join the dance and jump along.

And all one could hear is, "Cha-Cha-ouch – ribbet!"

Bailey the bunny pointed to each animal and started to count in English as Ricardo the rooster counted in Spanish:

one	-uno
two	-dos
three	-tres
four	-cuatro
five	-cinco
six	-seis
seven	-siete
eight	-ocho
nine	-nueve
ten	-diez
eleven	-once
twelve	-doce
thirteen	-trece
fourteen	-catorce
fifteen	-quince

The four amigos from South America made 15 new friends.

Can you count them in both English and Spanish?

The South American friends made fifteen new friends in America. Hasta la vista which means see you later!

www.ingramcontent.com/pod-product-compliance
Lightning Source LLC
LaVergne TN
LVHW070454080526
838202LV00035B/2824